What I Learned
On The Way
To The
Nursing Home

DORIS GATES

ISBN: 1480015709
ISBN-13: 978-1480015708

CONTENTS

Introduction

How many times have you heard comments like this, or said them about yourself?

"I will never let myself look like those old people I see hobbling around in the grocery store."

"I would rather be dead than look like that, or have to live in a nursing home."

"I told my kids to promise never to put me in one of those nursing homes."

"But... I'm so independent I will always be able to take care of myself!"

Yes, I too made remarks like that in the past and now I have had to eat my words. As the title of this book infers, I learned a lot before and after moving into a Nursing Home, and now I am naive enough to think I can change the world's negative opinions about Old Age and Group Living. Actually, if I can succeed in enlightening anyone about the enjoyment of their latter years, it is worth a try…especially if I can reach people *before* they're at the age which they have dreaded. And I also have a silent yearning to speak to people who are already in it. We have much in common.

The move to this facility has been the real test of a self-developed belief that "I could always find happiness wherever I lived". Of course, back then when I made that statement, I never pictured the "wherever" to be a nursing home. That realization began when I finally had to admit my age. That was a shock. I was like the majority of people who feel that after age fifty they need to apologize for being their age. Well, I have learned some new ways of thinking and seeing, and those new viewpoints show the beauty that these latter years can reveal. They can be very rewarding, and certainly not tragic like the old negative opinions that we are so used to.

Daily, I see more proof of the beauty that I might have missed if I had denied that my body was aging, and then had struggled to live at home alone. Now I know there are many modern places like this one that can provide a safer and happier way of life. As we go along I will share with you how my Happiness-Philosophy began and has progressed through the years.

CHAPTER 1

Vow of Happiness

To explain why I had such a strong belief in Happiness, it started two generations ago with my grandmother who then had the star role in the lives of all of her five children for as long as she lived. When my mother was 18 months old, her father (my Grandpa) died suddenly, leaving the family with no means of support. Immediately, Grandma became a single mother with four boys and one baby daughter to raise. To do that she worked day and night at her sewing machine making clothes for rich women in order just to feed, clothe and house her children.

There are many stories about all the hardships they suffered back at the turn of the century when life was much harsher than it is today. The four sons all went to work while still very young, then soon married and started their own families. That is when Grandma decided her working days were over and she became everyone's responsibility, and often reminded her children that she would always be their first responsibility—to take care of her for life. My mother, being the only girl, had the responsibility of living with her, while the sons' duty was to send money and visit often. They all did what they could but it was never enough to make

Grandma happy. She still had lots of energy and used it to keep dramatic episodes whirling around her constantly (just one of her ways to keep herself un-happy). The daughter, my mother, always lived with or near her and tried to make her happy, but it never worked.

As I was growing up I went along and tried to help in making her happy, but all efforts failed. Later I married and had a daughter named Hayden. Then as my mother aged, though she was different from and superior to Grandma in many ways, she began to repeat the same unhappy role that Grandma had suffered. It made me ask myself, "What if I am next to inherit that unhappy old-age pattern, and pass the burden of taking care of an unhappy mother (me) to my daughter?"

Even though Hayden was then only a child,

she understood the depressed-mother-problem because she experienced the same dreary atmosphere of Great Grandmother repeating in her Grandma. How could we avoid repeating this same condition in the future? We believed happiness was always possible, and that it was our responsibility to "see" it and "be" it. So from then on, when a problem would arise we vowed to remember to see the contrasting "good" in it, and save ourselves and others from the involvement of our possible depression.

Together we lived by the Vow of Happiness with good success. It helped us get through her growing up years, and my second marriage. We saw the blessings we received then, and any future changes that had to be made.

In time we both became independent and moved out on our own. She married and moved away and I became a single business woman. I started my own Interior Design business, then moved back to Little Rock to be near my elderly parents. Dad died shortly afterwards, and I had sole responsibility for Mother plus being the owner of my new business. During that time, I had physical problems like cancer and it took time to overcome that. During those years Mother was unhappy and finally had a severe stroke that took her life. By that time I was tired and ready for the blessing that followed: the offer to buy my business. I decided to take it and retire.

All during the twelve year back-home-in-Little-Rock era I was very involved in spiritual studies at the Unity Church here. Then after being retired I enjoyed having more time to study. After two years, Hayden urged me to move to California where she and her family were living. The possibility of living out there, plus being near them, sounded like a dream come true, so I moved and it was even better than I had imagined. However, after two years I decided L.A. was too big and too expensive for me to live there permanently. Besides, I really wanted to get back home to Little Rock.

At that exact time, my sister, Jeanne, was living in Hawaii and was very unhappy with her job. She invited me to move there to be near her— in another dream-location I couldn't resist. I thought I could afford such an adventure, so did it and gave myself another exciting Life Experience. That included the Problem before the Blessing of starting a design shop there which, from the beginning, everything about it went wrong.

Finally it seemed like I was failing the Happiness Vow and wanted to just give it up, but I couldn't leave the business because I had a five-year lease on the business space. Then of course the Blessing came, but it was in the form of a violent flash flood that washed down everything from the mountain above us, flooding the entire shop with mud; a heavenly escape because it made the lease become void, and soon I was un-crossing the Pacific ocean and reviewing some of the blessings Hawaii had given me. I had joined a group at the Unity Church where I studied *A Course in Miracles* which helped me tremendously as I struggled with the constant problems of the fatal business.

Back in Little Rock, moving into a nice apartment, starting counseling for former decorating clients, back at my old church organizing a study group - things went smoothly. Then, due to my eyesight problem, I had an accident totaling my new car and injuring myself and two passengers. My friend and daughter came to help but infuriated me by strongly advising I "quit driving". Rebelling...twice...I started to buy a new car anyway, but a very strong voice right in my ear said "NO!", so I gave up and went through a very difficult period of adjustment. Wonderful friends helped save my Happiness while NOT driving, and gave me more strength for the next episode.

Then there was a huge fire in my apartment building and every item I owned was smoke and water damaged. My wonderful friends were thankful for my belief in happiness; it made the whole ordeal of helping me move into another apartment at least a cheerful experience for everyone. So life was still good.

But how could I continue that optimism when the next tragedy struck! It was the sudden death of my only child, Hayden. How can one deal with such grief? But of course there was a gift even then—that was being able to talk to her from the Other Side. It happened as I was talking to Liz Voorhees on the telephone, she had a "connection" who was able to reach my very own Hayden herself, and that allowed us to have a real conversation together. She told me how wonderful she now felt and how beautiful everything was there, as only Hayden could express it. She talked about her dying experience and answered many of my questions about how life was there, which is so different from here. It took me a few days to be able to tell friends about it, I was so emotional. Since then Hayden and I have had more conversations and I am deeply rewarded knowing for sure that Life is Eternal...and it just increased my feeling of deep love for everyone. Thus the Vow of Happiness has continued, even after death!

All of this inspired me so much that I started writing my first book, *SUDDEN BOUTS OF HAPPINESS can Appear at the Worst of Times*. After finishing the book, my stamina just gave way and I needed full time help. So happiness did prevail again and my precious Adopted Family took charge of me and all of my affairs, including arrangements for my move to the nursing home. Friends...Friends! They seemed like the major factor in making my Happiness Vow work.

Looking back at our lives, it turns out that the original problem with the Mother/ Grandmother depression was truly a blessing to us because it made us start believing, then practicing, that Vow of Happiness. Their *unhappiness* made us look at the negative effect it caused for all the families involved. It gave us the will to reject old beliefs in being a victim, blaming others, and all the other so-called horrors of growing old. Actually both of the MOTHERS were loving and intelligent during a time in the world before all the changes of modern times had happened. I'll always love and respect them for all their efforts for good they caused, along with the problems they had to overcome.

When writing about my ups and downs, I know that many others have faced seemingly worse problems, and overcome them. But most have missed the joy of appreciating themselves for their own accomplishments, and the awareness of what they learned from their efforts. The purpose in reviewing my life was to show some of my problems, followed by the blessings I enjoyed when I allowed myself to <u>see</u> and learn from them. Life unfolds like a ladder with each rung containing a <u>learned lesson</u> to take you up to higher levels where you can see better. Please try to see what you have overcome through your every hardship, and how it made you strong. Now your body may show signs of wear...it's called *aging*...and that is a signal to make you proud for having lived through the experience.

CHAPTER 2

First Days of a New Life

I got the first look at my future home one cold December day. My friend, Alice, was taking me there for a preview so I could decide which of my accessories and furniture pieces would fit. When we first got outside of my apartment Alice seemed anxious about getting me get into her car because at that time I was extremely weak. Just then a stranger appeared and offered to help. He then lifted me up and got me settled into the car. As Alice and I drove away we laughed about the coincidence of a strong handsome man showing up at just the right time. Little did I know that in a short time we would meet again and become special friends (more later). Once more fate had smiled on me as I began to make another big life change.

We drove up to this beautiful building, parked and someone was there to help me get inside. Entering the Reception Area I noticed that the interior was as attractive as the exterior—very large, bright, cheerful and decorated just to suit my professional taste, and not depressing like I'd expected it would be.

We were welcomed and shown around by some of the friendly personnel. My new permanent quarters wouldn't be ready for several days but we looked at another one just like it so we could start planning what to bring that would fit.

The next day I actually moved into the nursing home "for good"…but in temporary quarters, still it was good. But I felt both pleased and fearful. Pleased because my Adopted Family would get a rest from looking after me at home since lately that responsibility had increased day after day. However, I was fearful that now, after getting me moved, they still have the job of clearing out my apartment and getting rid of all my furniture and other unneeded stuff. And after that, I'll still *always* need their attention and love. (Incidentally, when we all reach Heaven, you'll see some attractive women with diamonds in their haloes, then you'll know they are Dori's Adopted Daughters who deserve every one of the diamonds.)

As we walked down the clean shiny halls, old fears again popped up like... only a limited space for my "things"... most of them will have to go... and who will I be without those things? My adopted Family was already taking charge of clearing out or selling furnishings for this big life-change... it felt like it was eliminating ME. And, they were spending hours of hard work to accomplish this job. They said my responsibility was just to stay out of their way and to be happy when they called and told about another item they had sold. Since most of the buyers were friends, I was interested in who had bought what, and where my old furniture would live in the future.

I couldn't escape thinking that I had no 'future' and that this place was 'it' for the rest of my life. The finality of that thought was heavier than the reluctance of letting go of all my furniture. But, I offset that thought by remembering I would no longer have old worries either, like grocery shopping and cooking, house cleaning, safety, loneliness etc., so I said to myself: "Here comes a new way of life, Dori, and it is where you'll find your happiness from now on. Your job also is to show a cheerful face and optimistic outlook."

Scary, except in the back of my mind I knew that *whatever* future I experienced would be God-filled and loving. There is a purpose for every change and scary experience and, this one will be no exception (after I have gotten used to living with all these old people. like me). Then, negative feelings about them will change and *that will make me feel richer.*

The next day, the employees were helpful and anxious to take good care of me. It took a while to learn my way around and I met some of my neighbors by asking them questions. Later, we would get better acquainted, when I could begin to eat in the Dining Room. At first the idea of being "one of the group" hit another pang of reluctance and I appreciated the attitude of the Helpers here because they understood my reluctance and brought my meals to my room until I was ready to go out and eat with the others.

Physical therapy started immediately. It had a friendly and youthful atmosphere, and the professional staff helped heal my body and mind. My new room was soon ready to move into and made attractive with touches from the past. My habit of keeping an *awareness of good* developed from years of determination to find happiness through whatever happens. I wrote about it in my book "Sudden Bouts of Happiness" which shows that there is something good, funny, and beautiful in everything. So, what awareness will come to me in this new phase of living? Well, since it is Life, there will always be problems to face and overcome. Finish one of them, and Life gives us another one. Since I had already gone through some of the pain of aging, I assumed that now I knew all about latter day living… but being here showed me other aging souls going through more physical problems than I had ever encountered. I wanted to understand the divine purpose of these challenges that happen after living so long. It made me more aware of all the mysteries in Life while still seeing all the Love that surrounds all of us.

Early on, there was a place in my mind reserved for fear and worry. There I put having to face so many elders three times every day in the Dining Room, but soon it was time to quit eating alone in my room and join the other diners. There I found some improvements over my old negative mental picture. Materially, the Dining Room is very attractive and you are greeted with the good smell of food and the sight of many helpers busy satisfying the need for seating everyone and serving them their food. The diners are divided four to a table. It took a few days to get acquainted with my assigned tablemates. They were shy and quiet because they were held back by Alzheimer's. However, they had loving family members who joined them for daily meals and I enjoyed their company and didn't suffer from lack of conversation for very long. Finally, I also had some conversation with those at other tables. It was mostly complaints about everything…but at least it was talking and somehow that in itself was a comfort. Too much positive talk would not have been as appropriate as sharing a little "ain't it awful?" and "why don't they?" Such complaining can bring shy people together at first. And very soon I found close friends with new avenues of conversation, and the place became homey and warm.

One day, a tablemate and I were having a discussion on the subject of Death. She told me about a time when she was extremely depressed and sick, and decided it was her time to die. She thought *she* would do the deed herself, so by just closing her eyes and giving the command, she simply waited for it to happen. Nothing happened so she gave up and is still living. I felt the subtle humor of the situation and a deep shared closeness to this still-alive friend.

After getting better acquainted with more people, conversations did begin to happen, and that family feeling started and that is the purpose of daily dining together. Here we can face our mortality, our successes and failures, and send our compassion and love out to the world. Happy conversations carry more smiles and are contagious, and one day we might end up with full belly-laughs.

After a few weeks of eating three times a day in the Dining Room, I realized that I felt love for every person there, including the staff and relatives visiting their loved ones. Where else could I have such a family experience? So, you can see how my negative feelings have disappeared and now I live with interesting people who have a variety of backgrounds and dispositions and handicaps… not your common eating place, but always unique.

CHAPTER 3

Facing Life Changes

Don't let my positive attitude fool you. The changes we face when entering a nursing home can be major. Unless you served in the Armed Forces there is nothing to compare it to. The privacy of your regular home is gone (forever). You are confined to a small space with just room for personal necessities. Even though the atmosphere of the whole building is beautiful and you are given loving attention from a talented medical staff and activities director, the "change ain't fun"! It's a big change, so at first you must be patient, start counting your blessings *immediately*, and notice how quickly you can actually SEE them take place.

If you came here straight from a stay in the hospital, the shock of Group Living may be slightly less, *and* if you are a Positive Thinker and love to study Life Experiences, you'll find plenty to occupy your interest here right away. It's a different experience, just like all the other changes in your life were.

At first you may not see the blessings here… like the welcoming attention you get day and night, and all the other services that are done to make you happy and feel important. As I watch people come in, unsure and frightened, I can see them gradually change back to their original charm and renewed health. It is important to *see* things change for the better, then pass that vision on to others. It helps everyone the world over to hear about the good things that await them in their latter years. Your complimentary remarks about nursing homes may help soothe some fearful opinions the general public holds against them.

The dreadful reputation of nursing home life that is embedded in the minds of most elderly people makes them so biased that no matter what life improvements are offered, they cannot accept them. They feel compelled to fight against old age and themselves for requiring this kind of care. Many act as though they are unfairly cast into a dungeon with wild animals, and they must fight their way out of it. The fight is from real fear of this change which had to be addressed for their good and for the relief of people close to them who can no longer give them the kind of care that is required.

It is hard to let go of personal possessions and a reputation of independence and power. Some learn that such things are no longer needed and begin to see different advantages for themselves and their family. Some never make the change of mind for the better, and suffer the consequences of unhappiness both for themselves and their family.

For new residents and everyone in your outside family, here is a process you can begin to understand that will be helpful. There is a reluctance many of us feel toward having to receive all the care we require at this time in the Game of Life. When we begin to recognize and respect the purpose of this Game, we'll better understand the way much of life works for both the young and the old.

The Game requires at least two people, a GIVER and a RECEIVER, and I call it the Giving/Receiving Process. The part that one plays as a Giver may be more familiar to you. Giving is sweeter and more satisfying than having to receive. In this particular game, the Giver is usually one who is 'on their feet', younger, is still able to drive, and is more at home out in the business world.

Try now to understand the part played by and called the RECEIVER. That part is less appealing because being in it doesn't give much self-satisfaction. However, that part is necessary for this Life Game to run efficiently. In this case it applies to the elderly because they have become unable to handle certain matters alone, and many times find it difficult to face that fact, and don't give much appreciation to their Givers. When the Givers are our own family members, we consider them "trying to help because they think I don't have good sense any more". That is a hard position to have to face, especially for anyone's ego, but we have to blame someone. Outsiders see our so-called "Bossy Givers" as kind-hearted helpers who must face angry Receivers who are afraid of losing authority over their finances, health and very existence.

I, myself, am trying to be a grateful Receiver, and it is interesting to watch my own inner ego-responses when I have to receive, even when I know it is the name of the Game. I have found that if I call it just what it is, the Giving/Receiving Game, it helps even if it causes some depression. When that happens, I try to remember to turn around and give thanks for my wonderful, intelligent Givers, and follow their advice because I know that they have the good sense, and love, and devotion… all the qualities that will send them straight to Heaven (and I want to be there with them).

Even after learning how to deal with the Receiving part, my body continued its natural aging, and I realized there was plenty more learning to do. That is, facing the fact that eighty-eight year old bodies wear out and physically decline. Here's where the story can turn ugly if one becomes depressed and sees their present situation as unfair, sad and lonely. Even though my body might have become fragile, I knew I must look for and see the compensations that will be mine for living this full span of years.

Jumping ahead two years to now when I am ninety, and no longer eighty-eight, and again I still had this question: "At this age what has been the advantage of me living these last two years?" Then I stopped and thought of all of the opportunities for "soul growth" these two years here at the Nursing Home have given me, like the opportunity to associate with many different types of people. It's a larger circle here than any of us would have had when living alone. By soul growth, I mean lessons learned that become permanent for the soul (like rising above dependence and fascination for material possessions, and adjusting my People Pleasing obsession...these are permanent lessons that will remain with me thru eternity).

Going through a lifetime of living on this plateau is a gift because this is the best place to change errors you carry from past lives. Such speculation brings on a truer self-evaluation. Also sharing your memories with family and friends can surprise you as they seem to enjoy hearing about your past - and it accents the warm world of love and humor that can be ours to live in. You must allow more people in your life. There is a tendency for elderly people to rely on one person to fill all their needs, and that one person can become exhausted. Remember there are others who have talents and the desire to give, so accept more of their attention and learn to be a more grateful Receiver.

If I do my transition well, I must give credit to my wonderful Adopted Family who understood the shock when I lost my only child. They relieved some of my emptiness as they valiantly stepped in, filling my many needs. Their ages are closer to my deceased daughter's age and it kept our communication at a younger level (for my benefit). I want to tell more about each of them in genuine and complimentary description but have to wait because I start to sound like a bragging mother.

For years, my group of Givers has studied inspiring books with me twice a month at my home. Now we meet in my different kind of "home" here at Briarwood. By attending our Study Group here on a regular basis, they get to see first-hand how acceptable old-age living can be, and even happy. They can spread that good news to others, and it might relieve outsiders of some unnecessary worry about their own future.

CHAPTER 4

Embarrassments

Well, you've read about my trauma of having to eat three times a day with other older people seen as sick in body and mind. And then, how soon I liked everyone and appreciated the honor of sharing this last phase of our lives together in this loving and beautiful environment.

I also had to undergo another change from the old, regular way of living and that was in bathing my body, which required moving it from a wheelchair to the shower, safely. I admit my resistance to exposing my nude body to anybody, but it had to be done with the help of an assistant. The assistant was the saving grace in this whole embarrassing routine. I hadn't had my body washed by anyone except my mother when I was an infant. Naturally, I'd forgotten the luxury of capable hands soaping down all of my body, rinsing it, and then drying it with a big soft towel. This was followed by helping me dress and get settled back into my wheelchair. It was only embarrassing at first and I must admit how luxurious the ceremony became after a few times.

During the procedure it was interesting to overhear conversations going on in the other three stalls of the shower room. I heard one lady say to her shower assistant, "Be careful, don't touch me there! That part of my body belongs to my husband." (Very personal and funny at the same time.)

Another remark, in the form of advice, came from an assistant while helping someone get dressed and pull up her pants. The subject of their conversation was "which is more proper, slacks or shorts?" The assistant advised, "Now honey, it's alright for you to let men see your bare legs, even up a little above your knee. Men like that, but don't let them see any further up because seeing any higher up can make men go blind."

Outside in the hallway, another unforgettable remark was picked up. My friend, Mary Ellen, was walking down the hall and passed a resident sitting in a wheelchair, and casually said to her, "Hello, how are you?" and the reply was, "I was just fine, until I got <u>old</u>."

Here's another embarrassment you may have had when answering to someone's greeting in question "How are you?" and your answer left you feeling embarrassed. It happened to me one morning when I really didn't feel well and a friend passed by with a "Hello, how are you?" That morning, I couldn't resist answering *honestly* to the question saying, "I don't feel well at all, couldn't sleep last night and woke up with this sinus headache and…" (Suddenly, I realized I had lost eye contact with my friend, and she seemed to be busy brushing a bit of lint from her sleeve). I wished I could retrieve my honest words from the air and then quickly moved out of her sight, but I couldn't. I had to stay, and so I closed our meeting with this lie, "…but I feel fine now, how are you?" She correctly answered, "Fine thanks." and walked away.

For a while the embarrassment hurt, and then I forced myself to think about the incident. Finally, I discovered that there was only ONE correct answer to that common (how are you?) question. It is (and always was) correct to just answer "Fine". That's because the question has nothing to do with your present physical condition. From now on, I will always remember that the greeting implies "How are you – mentally?" Then it is not a lie to answer that you are fine (mentally) because you really are... and saying it out loud helps to prove to yourself that you are, and always will be, mentally _fine, great and wonderful_.

CHAPTER 5

Tears

Recently I saw a friend's tear-streamed face and it made me review my own experience and explain my lack of ability to shed tears when I feel an emotion of either sadness or happiness. Is that a handicap or a blessing? I caused it to happen to me many years ago when newly divorced and very unhappy at times about being single, so there were plenty of times to be depressed and ending up in tears. Not the attractive kind, but the sobbing, swollen red eyes, sniffing nose crying session followed by an exhausting headache. That is what I beheld when seeing my face in the mirror, and I was more devastated than ever.

The mirror reflection made me ask myself if any problem was serious enough to cause me to look that bad. I answered, " NO!!!, nothing is worth such suffering." Then I cried some more, went to the bathroom, washed my face, looked in the mirror again and saw the damage it reflected, and said out loud, "Never again will I allow myself to cry tears again." I really meant it...and that remark probably changed my future for the better.

For the past thirty years the total amount of my tears might fill 2 or 3 teaspoons. Now, no amount of anger, sadness, fear, or love really causes me to cry tears. I do still have those same strong emotions, and when they happen I feel a tingling around my eyes and a need to blow my nose, then after calming down I see the whole picture a little differently and start looking for better solutions that won't mess up my face, and give me a headache.

All of my friends probably think I am heartless, or weird, and that I'd be better off after a good cry. They insist that crying makes them feel better (and their faces probably held up better than mine did after crying). Some authorities also recommend a (good) cry because it helps to get rid of the bad feelings you are holding deep inside. But after looking at both sides and reviewing all my non-crying years, I have to personally disagree.

After my commitment to stop shedding tears, the same old emotional feelings continued, but I realized that I truly could not shed tears about anything any more...so gradually I found other methods that would not harden my heart toward other people, but actually would make my heart softer.

These new ways began to improve my day to day living. When the upsets happened I had to stop and slow down my breathing which enabled me to see a clearer picture of the upset and let me feel my pain. That clearer viewpoint allowed me the space in time to gain more understanding of the event and the people in it. This brought healing to personal problems much quicker and without the whirl of sobbing in self-pity and resentment toward whatever I might have believed caused the problem. So over the years it has allowed me time for more enjoyable activities and I am grateful for the non-crying decision I made so long ago.

P.S. I am not recommending this type of self-hypnosis-against-tears for anyone else. This review was needed for me, it just seemed unusual and worth repeating.

CHAPTER 6

Blame

Get ready to look at another way of using your Mind. In previous chapters, we learned that *observing our thoughts is not an easy habit to acquire.* Yet, we have also discovered that there are more riches available for us when we can keep expanding the treasure located right there in the head. After you start to become aware of what you're thinking, you will finally begin to *hear* those thoughts *before* they come out of your mouth. Start now trying to remember to listen when you're in conversation about things, or people you say are at fault. You may be surprised to hear yourself issuing more *complaints* than you had imagined. Complaining is just an old enjoyable habit, so you probably get comfort hearing others cast blame for their troubles. But blaming is as harmful in solitude as it is when spoken out loud to others.

Now you may ask, "What's wrong with complaining or listening to complaints? Isn't it just speaking the truth about all the things that are so wrong, or naming the person and how they caused the problem? Answer: *Well, see it this way, it was only your reasoning that figured out who or what was to blame, and such thinking simply doesn't go far enough to find the greater truth about the problem.*

This type of reasoning began in childhood when we were fearful of getting in trouble, like for hitting someone or breaking something. So, we quickly found someone or something to blame it on in an attempt to save ourselves from punishment. As adults, we still find this childish trick a handy solution for any problem that bothers us.

Just watch how we use Blame. See how it puffs us up and makes us feel superior! Yes, and after all, we think we are pretty smart to "find the guilty one". In the past, we have found many subjects we called the "Problem-Causers". The guilty ones varied from the boss, our spouse, the city or federal government, the weather, the nursing home - all easy targets that we have made to bare the blame so we could feel better about ourselves.

I personally went through some of that until I started observing my thoughts and remembering conversations of the past. It made me <u>not feel so superior</u> about those words I had spoken loud and clear. And worse, I noticed how often I did it. After starting to really listen first to the sounds in my head, it killed the old comfortable feeling I once had righteously enjoyed. Where was all the satisfaction then? It was gone! Before, when there was a problem, I truly believed there was only one way to solve it, and that was to announce who was to *blame* and let it be known.

It is a bitter pill to swallow, but I must admit that I was an example of using that kind of judgment. I remember the words I used when telling how my ex-husband was to blame for the break-up of our marriage. Finally, that kind of announcement started making me feel guilty, and then I had to admit to myself that blaming him was not the whole truth. I began seeing some of the *truth* about the divorce and had to admit he was still the same nice man I'd once married. The separation became necessary as we both had changed through the years and both needed the freedom of divorce. Now, seeing the truth about that situation, without blaming him or feeling guilty about old mistaken judgments, I enjoy just feeling lighter because I understand all such situations better now.

When you can exchange <u>blame</u> for <u>understanding</u>, then spiritual learning begins. Later, when you hear yourself expressing those blaming statements, you can get another look at your old self-righteousness and begin to ask yourself if all your old opinions were fair. This process of looking at our words is only possible after we begin to take time to quiet the chatter in our minds. In those few seconds you'll slow down, and so maybe will your criticism, and you will be able to uncover more understanding of the situation. Repeat the slowdown habit as often as possible before speaking!

When successful, you will finally feel lighter inside because you have risen above pettiness and have a new feeling of peace born within you. This may be a feeling you didn't even know you *wanted*. You always thought it was more desirable to be the *winner* by proclaiming that your *opponent* was wrong. Now, that kind of judgment has changed, and a new feeling of peace rises up. It doesn't feel like *weakness* from losing a battle, but *strength* from rising up with a greater understanding of your opponent, and observing a better world. Taking time to still the mind sets up greater order in your thinking, not only for problems involving people, but for other things like politics, business, history - just a few thought-provoking topics that give you time to see more sides of a situation before making judgments.

You may have heard of the *Course in Miracles.* I studied it for many years and it helped me to gradually quit looking for the errors in a situation. It made me began to feel more "at one" with my opponent instead of separate (with one person being right and the other wrong). Looking at everyone's actions, without placing guilt on myself or the other, allowed a deeper look at what had actually happened.

Getting ego (the feeling of separation) out of the way prepares for greater blessings. You may begin to see yourself *at one* with people you used to be *at war* with. All of this may be more far-reaching than shows up right now. As you practice Oneness, notice your inner feeling of lightness and peace. Such feelings can spread throughout the world, carrying more personal respect for every man, woman, child, black, white, brown, yellow. This requires you to stop blaming and start taking on the gift of understanding, both for yourself and the world.

So what does this optimistic feeling about Life mean to people here at the nursing home? Most older people believe they don't have that much time left to begin mind-changing ideas. Can't you hear them say, "Why bother with that stuff at my age!?" Well, I learned and gained more from mind-changing *after middle age.* Now it is making me free of old nagging thoughts I was once burdened with... like fear, anger, victimhood. It is never too late to change old negative thinking patterns to positive beliefs. If you need a role model to help you practice such new thinking, find one, (and you may eventually become one). Think how your success at living happily during the latter phase of your life will change those around you! It begins to change the people where you live after seeing the glow of your joy. Your family & friends may proudly join your optimism and spread the good news of your happiness endlessly throughout the world.

All of this is even more important for the younger generation. Young people have more remaining years to practice Understanding and Oneness than older relatives have. Know that none of us need to have the kind of Old Age we hear so direly predicted. If you hear yourself joining in those fears, remember it need not be the truth for anyone's future. After you change the way you <u>see</u> Life, you won't worry about your latter years and, through your eyes, family members will see how their lives can be better.

CHAPTER 7

The Blessing of Forgetting

Just a few weeks after becoming "one of them" (a resident), I did the worst thing a resident can do here, besides dying, and it was to fall down. It was early morning and I rushed to the closet to grab my robe so I'd be decent to go to breakfast. But, in my sleepiness and hurry, I stepped out of bed to walk without my walker (a thing to never, ever do again). A walker is like a part of your body to support you when up on your feet, but I forgot, and crashed my head on this cold concrete floor; a very hard lesson to have to learn. My skull was badly bruised and my elbow broken. So for months, with my arm in a cast, I was one-handed, confined to a wheelchair and had to have help constantly. That was frustrating enough, but worse were the lectures from every person who saw me or helped me here in the building. Without humor or sympathy they just reminded me to be more careful (as if in this condition I needed reminding!). But maybe I did, because, so far, I do remember to go slower and always have something near to hold me up.

Another emergency occurred some time later, when I was hospitalized again with a serious bout of pneumonia. Since then, I put those episodes out of my mind so successfully that when I needed the dates of them, I had only a faint memory of when both happened, so had to search thru many journal pages to find them. Then, I became concerned that such recent events had left my mind so soon. Was it a memory weakness that caused me to forget the injured skull and broken elbow? Should I be less quick to wipe unpleasant events like that from my mind? Being a people-pleaser, I notice that people don't enjoy hearing about your past illnesses, so to fix that I simply erase the details of unpleasant events (like sickness) from my thinking so I don't run the risk of boring anyone.

I used to keep a little notebook in my purse, and made notes of all the details I needed to remember. It saved me time and trouble when I couldn't remember names or numbers. Now my friends, Rebecca and Alice, take care of bill paying and appointments so I don't have to bother keeping the notebook always by my side. Now, as a care-free retiree, should I worry about my loss of memory?

A very surprising idea once came to my attention and it was this: The ability to <u>forget is a blessing!</u> That's quite a comfort to someone like me who always had felt inferior to people who could quote verbatim from poems and quotes and remember names of everyone they ever met. But back to the Blessings of Forgetting, think how it relates to *forgiveness.* A hurtful incident isn't really forgiven until you can *forget it.* Think about the common remark… "I might forgive someone but I just can never forget it"… or when someone offended you and remembered it so strongly that they later apologized for it. But, you had forgotten the offense completely and could not even remember what it was… all that time you had enjoyed a mind free from remembering simple thoughtless mistakes... another advantage of forgetting. An elderly person must remember the Blessings of Forgetting when he or she occasionally forgets something. Loss of memory *can* be a serious symptom of certain illnesses, but *choosing* to forget some boring detail is healthy and makes good sense.

Human forgetting reminds me of the story of a woman caught here racing down the hall in a wheelchair so fast she almost collided with a nurse and her medicine cart. The nurse was irritated, "Slow down, honey, where are you going in such a big rush?" The lady answered, "Down to Myrtle's office." The nurse asked, "Why must you get there so fast?" She replied, "If I don't go fast I might forget where I'm going."

CHAPTER 8

Learning by Listening

Until recently, I thought people didn't listen because they weren't interested in what other people were saying. Now that I have lost some of my own hearing, I have a better understanding of the seriousness of a hearing loss. Now I can see the general lack of empathy shown by those who *can* still hear for those with hearing loss. It is hard to understand how the loss of hearing affects the personality and life of those so handicapped, until your own hearing starts to recede. With age, my hearing has become weaker, even when wearing costly hearing aids. Needless to say, now I am more tolerant of the ones who have to ask someone to repeat what they just said. I remember my old lack of understanding when my Mother's feelings were hurt when people didn't speak loud enough for her to hear them.

Some people are embarrassed and try to cover up their deafness by just avoiding conversations. Now I know how isolated one can feel around conversational groups when their lack of responses may give the group the impression that they just aren't interested. So I suggest that you let it be known that you can't hear, but try to pay special attention to people anyway.

So, how can we retain our "happiness" if our hearing gets worse? Well of course, it helps if you are already equipped with other interests like art and handicrafts, reading, sports (to mention a few). Then, losing the pleasure of hearing won't ruin your joy. You can compensate by watching others more closely and paying more attention to their lives and stories. Admit your hearing loss, but don't expect people to be able to change their volume or phrasing permanently when speaking in ordinary conversation voice. I couldn't do that when I tried, even to please my Mother whom I loved. Through it all, try to keep your focus on Happiness and Love for everyone... that opens many doors with compensating surprises.

Here is a story of someone who seemed to have no interest or the curiosity to listen to any voice but his own. It is about an elderly man who lived in my same apartment complex. We were both in the laundry room waiting for clothes to dry. He was telling me about the time he fell off his roof. While listening, I raised up to reach the dryer and hit my head on it with a blow so hard that blood started running down on my face. The "storyteller" saw it but continued telling me his story. I finally had to stop listening and leave, "I'm sorry to interrupt you but I have to go home and bandage this injury that you must have seen when I hit the dryer with my head." His only closing remark was, "Too bad for you to have to leave and miss the end of my story about falling off the roof." Was his problem lack of hearing or seeing, or was he so intent on telling his own story that he closed himself off to anyone else? Helen Keller said the only thing worse than being blind is having *sight but no vision*... same with having hearing but being unable to listen.

There is great value in being a good listener

in a world where there are so few. Good listeners seem to be happier and warmer than their opposites. Practice real listening when you are young, then later, when your body slows down and listening has become a habit, you will have the means to save yourself from boredom and loneliness. Try to gain more curiosity in what others have to say and you will by-pass hearing only one voice... your own. Find good entertainment in listening to other people's stories and you will gain plenty of wisdom and humor throughout your latter years. It will foster a more loving heart and an appreciation of life.

If a child's ideas are not heard or considered, the child may feel undervalued, and grow into adulthood feeling unloved and unworthy. *Listening is an act of love.* It isn't always a shared activity, especially among the aged. Here at the

Home, communication between residents was difficult at first, and would have been worse for me if I hadn't had the staff of caretakers here to talk with. Their loving attention to everyone helps make up for any lack of communication between residents. Problems are caused because many residents are hard of hearing and that brings on loneliness and depression which can even cause physical problems. But as the saying goes, "Old age is not for sissies". That's why it's so important to learn as much as possible about keeping up your social skills <u>now</u>. If you don't, when you yourself are elderly, you could be very needy for the attention of whoever is around... and no one may want to give it to you because you had kept yourself *separate* and not interested in giving attention and listening. Practice curiosity and real listening <u>now</u> and you'll likely find happiness and humor wherever you are. You may be surprised at the good nursing care you will receive here and how your health can even improve. Remember the days and long nights when you were alone in your home and how hard it was for family and friends to look after you all the time. Yet finding the right people to work in your home was a big responsibility so, hopefully, you cherish your new life. New freedom and lack of responsibilities can be a blessing as you enjoy needed rest, and time to read new books and review old ones. Why do so many people picture this lifestyle as unacceptable instead of the gift of freedom that it is? *Because it un productive looks like NTSS, sed, lonely*

Back to learning the art of listening, it is important to learn to listen to your thoughts. When I first came here I continued to stay busy non-stop, thinking I was avoiding boredom and loneliness. I had bought into the popular belief that slowing down was a dreadful way to live. When I was tired and wanted to rest, I would recall a funny remark repeated by an old TV comedian: "Remember when you get old, don't make the mistake of falling in love *with your bed*". I would smile and stay busy following the old work ethic. Finally, my body became consumed with tiredness and the desire to take naps. Since I was learning to listen to my thoughts, I actually heard the word "rest", and then laughed as it was connected to "home"... Rest Home. Isn't that what we used to call the place where older people went to get much needed rest? Yes, so I respectfully do just that.

CHAPTER 9

Thinking Can Make It So

Sometimes, do you wonder if happiness is a GIFT that others receive just because they are lucky? Or, because they come from the right family? Or, are simply being favored by God? NOT TRUE! Happiness can be a major personal accomplishment brought on by one's THOUGHTS, and few people realize it's their own <u>thinking</u> that makes them happy or miserable.

But how do you change the way you think? Well, first you must be able to observe your own thoughts. That requires quieting some of the old thoughts racing around in the mind. So stop a moment now and try to *see* what your thoughts are. Start by making the body very still, take three deep slow breaths. Now think about a *worry* you carry... see a mental picture of it. Is it happening now or in the future? More frequently, worries are set in the future. So it has not actually happened.

With your own creative imagination, you have designed a picture of what might happen. That *made-up picture in your mind* is causing pain, anxiety, and physical problems, which can be *contagious* to everyone who lives around you. Would you like to destroy those worrisome illusions? Some people want to hold onto their own fearful picture because, to them, it proves that they are important to the people they worry about... and also shows their love and willingness to sacrifice their own happiness just for them. If you're not in that category, and are serious about opening your mental door and experiencing new viewpoints, you don't have to destroy all your old opinions. Just put them on a back burner while you observe, critically, another side of the fear that you always believed was real. Many people are so stubborn they can't see a new truth that can change old fearful, depressing beliefs. Making a <u>change</u> requires courage to step out, maybe for the first time, and allow yourself to experience a better, healthier lifestyle... with the happiness you've always deserved.

What does "Opening Up Your Thought-Power" mean to people who are already in the latter years of their lifespan? This is the time when the body slows down and you have more time alone with old memories and new painful physical changes to deal with. Investigating your thoughts could give you a new opportunity to see how dark and negative some of those old thoughts were. You can look at examples of people who are suffering from their old wrong opinions... like believing that their age makes them unattractive, that health problems are serious death threats, that children never appreciate parents, only the rich can enjoy life, etc. etc. etc. Eliminating that kind of thinking can be a tonic for a happier "old age" or for any age. Healthy thinking contributes to making everything around the world better.

Now you may be curious and ready to watch your thoughts just to see how many are filled with fear. When I started watching my thinking I was astonished at the large amount of fear I pictured in my mind constantly, like fear of failure, fear of showing my ignorance, fear of bodily pain, fear of sickness - all imagined concerns I thought might happen at any minute. Seeing these thoughts made me want to start finding ways to change them. I eagerly studied creative ideas of people like Thomas Edison and Bill Gates. They had great curiosity and the tenacity to stay with an idea until its successful end, making this world a greater place in which to live. And Albert Einstein said, "Imagination is more important than knowledge." All inventions began in someone's mind that was *not bogged down in fear.* There are still some fears to eliminate and I constantly guard the mental contents of my brain. Not yet in a creative category like Edison, I have created happiness even living in a nursing home. Left unchanged in an old fear-filled mind, I could have ended up suffering anxiety, fear, resentment…and believing that my problems were the Truth.

It is not easy to observe your thoughts, try it for a few seconds…that's as long as most concentration will last without an assignment to focus on. Here's one to start with and you can treat it like a game. Take a blank sheet of lined paper and across the top write: "Naming the Fears as They Cross My Mind". Start each sentence with "I am afraid of…" and fill in the blank space quickly by naming whatever fear pops into your mind. I did this assignment once and was surprised how quickly the page was filled, and how honest I felt about its contents. Many fears seemed so minor that I laughed at them. But even though silly, at least I was learning to see my fears and realize how wasted some were. Others looked serious and seeing them in my own writing made me want to start seeing what changes were needed while giving more respect to my mind.

Seeing thoughts more clearly, you will get a better view of past concerns. Of course, you remember the pain and worry they caused, but can you find the blessings that followed the problem afterwards? Maybe not. This is probably a new process for your thinking and just waiting to be manifested by you. I step out on a limb and assure you there are blessings everywhere in your life.

After worrying and struggling for years about a problem, later you will see how the whole episode brought on a present blessing. I thought my greatest handicap was not finishing a formal education. For years, I felt embarrassed and lacked self-confidence. Finally I started *observing* those painful thoughts in a different way because I was weary of thinking they were the Truth. I made myself begin to look at the advantages of my *Self*-education. It has been a joyful activity all of my adult life and gave me more of the "common sense" that came through experience than a college diploma would have provided. Does this remind you of some painful regret from the past that you were carrying? As you let it go, you will find that there are blessings that remain… ones that could not have been possible without first having had the problem. Seeing it now will show you what this problem taught you. Reviewing the path that you take while changing viewpoints will help you learn how to appreciate future problems. Now, I watch as any new personal problem unfolds and anticipate the blessing it will surely give me. After you become aware of all the good you receive, even during troubling times, you will see Divine Goodness pouring into all of creation.

Troubles and the realizations of their purpose in life are powerful motivators. This can free one from morbid fantasies and reveal the Greater Truth. You may not be able to convince "oldsters" of that unless they are willing and capable of seeing all their own blessings, past and present. *The unconscious mind seems to want to hold onto old fears and worries about anything pertaining to the future.* Even when planning a pleasant future event, dark pictures of possible failure and embarrassment can take hold of the mind... sometimes accompanied by faster

When someone insults you or trys to make you look like its stupid because they feel stupid not worthy says more about them Do not respond

78

heartbeat and uneven breathing. All this becomes more serious as we age. That is why it is so important for older people (in fact, people of any age) to keep their minds open to better ways of seeing. Don't give up. *It is never too late (and it never too early) to embrace new ideas that will improve your life and add permanent happiness.*

I mentioned in Chapter One about the handsome stranger who lifted me into Alice's car the day she was taking me to see this nursing home for the first time. Little did I know we would meet again someday and become special friends. Since then, I was so busy getting adjusted to the new life here at the Home that I never thought about the possibility of ever meeting him again - especially the possibility that someone so much younger and attractive would bother to meet a nursing home "freshman" like me. But I knew it could be just another example of the nice surprises that are always lurking around the corner. Well, it happened when I least expected it one morning as I was getting my hair done. One of the assistants came into the hair salon and told me that there was a man in my room waiting to see me. Not wanting whoever it was to have to wait until my hair was dry, I quickly put on a shower cap and went back to my room. At first, I didn't recognize him and he had to remind me of where it was that we first met. We had a nice short conversation and made plans to meet again soon. (Later he told Alice he was impressed with me that day for not apologizing for the state of my hair.) That meeting led to more visits and interesting conversations... he is very spiritually minded and so am I, and it was a time when we both needed to share inspirations. He always brought me flowers or a bakery treat, which was noticed by the observers around here. It was fun to keep them interested since, to them, I called him "my Boyfriend". After a few months, I didn't see him as often. Then about the time of my birthday he sent me a card with a beautiful note describing our spiritual relationship. It was a gift I will always treasure.

Soon afterward he came by with a very attractive lady he wanted me to meet. I could tell from her remarks that they were a serious romantic couple soon to be married. I was very glad he had a suitable partner. At the same time, I knew I would miss seeing him as often (and my ego would miss getting to show him off and brag about having a Boyfriend at my age).

A few years ago I was cured from the obsession that so many single females carry in their minds... it is called "Finding Mr. Right". Family and friends shared this belief and urged me if I'd try harder I could find HIM and we all would live happily ever after. My attempts were half-hearted but when I lived in California, it almost happened. There I met a prospective "Mr. Right" and the search seemed to be concluding. Soon it seemed appropriate to live together in a kind of trial-marriage. Fortunately it was just a "Trial" because the break-up happened after only six months. By then I had become so trapped in that faux-marriage that I was ready to have a nervous break-down. So I left, and immediately became aware of the blessing of it all. My mind was forever cured of the Search for Mr. Right and I could appreciate the rest of my life as a happy single person, enjoying male friendships without the requirement that they make my life perfect.

That was just an example of an older person learning a better way of <u>seeing.</u> Some people are never able to really <u>see</u> that better way. Thankfully, I could learn a lesson with the awareness it was "better late than never".

CHAPTER 10

Wisdom through Writing

Have you ever considered getting to know yourself better? Or, that you might enjoy having a conversation just by yourself? Start getting to know yourself better thru writing. The sacred thoughts you are capable of expressing take time and effort to put on paper. You may say, "Well, I just never had that ability to write down what I was thinking and I'm afraid it's too late to start now. Besides, since

I'm not all that wise, I would be too embarrassed for anyone to see what I wrote."

Years ago, I too had some timidity that prevented me from writing my thoughts in a journal. Then, when attending a class, the teacher challenged us to start keeping a notebook and write our own prayers in it every day for the next thirty days. Hesitant to begin, but eager to overcome my shyness about writing, I took the challenge and did it. In so doing that, I not only gained more respect for my writing ability, but also learned about the power of my own prayers.

Afterwards with new confidence I began a regular habit of keeping a personal journal. Having already become aware of my thoughts, now I could actually *review* them. It is a great way of seeing, in writing, the truth about questions you previously couldn't answer. This becomes a comfort because now you are not alone when you need to talk about a situation that bothers you. Journaling is a step beyond "talking to yourself" because it gives you the resources of a wise voice from the *unseen world* that talks to you. Please try writing when you are disturbed and need to work through an issue. Then you'll have a clearer picture of the situation so you can deal with it. Also write when you feel greatly inspired and want to remember it, if your journal isn't handy, any piece of paper will do. It may be appropriate to pray first because you need to ask Holy Spirit for more guidance. After you write your thoughts, then read what was written, and think about it, then write more as new insights come up.

A common worry is about keeping your writing private. To date, I have not heard reports of anyone actually having that invasion of privacy. Would-be invaders are more interested in their own affairs and can't be bothered with reading about yours (even if you asked them to). Just don't overdo talking to the wrong person about your new writing project… it might entice a snooper. So keep your journal out of the sight of anyone. Thru the past years I have filled twenty-two personal journals and no one has ever shown any interest in reading them. If you can't keep a journal because of the risk (embarrassment, invasion of privacy, etc.), just keep writing anyway… and destroy instead of saving it. Simply writing your own thoughts then reviewing them is beneficial, but sad to destroy good memories.

This writing habit may also be appealing to older people since they have priceless knowledge and memories that only they can pass on to younger generations. Let them know how many people would value this information. This retirement age provides the perfect time to create gifts in scrapbook form. It is also a joy to sort through old pictures and tell stories about them of olden times that others love to hear. If preparation for the job gets too heavy for you, the storyteller, it could be a loving time to get help from a grandchild or friend.

The time has come to start celebrating the years of life an elderly person has come thru, not mainly because they might still look or act young, but because of their years of experience and the lessons it has taught them. Don't let these stories be lost because of the obsessions with the worship of youth. Remember as you write about your life, good or bad, young or old, the gift is in seeing the beauty of Living a Life. Writing is so valuable at any age; see it educating you and making you less hesitant to express your own thoughts.

CHAPTER 11

Way To Go

I am reminded of my friend Mary Ann's mother and how her attitude of fun made life more acceptable for herself and family. Mary Ann and her husband, Mal, looked forward to having her move into their home so they could share her pleasant personality for the rest of her life. They remodeled part of their house to make her comfortable, and everything went well for several years. Then Mother's physical body broke down and the only solution seemed to find the ideal nursing home for her. Mary Ann was very depressed because of the upcoming move, and spent long days searching the area until she found just the most suitable place.

The move happened and it was perfect because Mother seemed so happy there. It was a surprise to everyone that it worked so well and they credited it mainly to her mother's positive attitude about her new environment. She made friends easily (even one boyfriend) and she enjoyed many of the social activities there, mainly card playing. Mary Ann didn't expect Mother to adapt so quickly to a nursing home life... she missed having her mother at home with her, and she was the one who had to adjust to the change. Mother adjusted quickly to her new home with plenty of friendly people always available for a card game. It suited her personality very well... she just loved people and enjoyed being one of them, whether in a daughter's home or in a place that specialized in taking care of more physical needs. After many months in that environment the mother passed away. Mary Ann and Mal grieved at their loss, but were comforted by pleasant memories of having had her in their home, then finding another home for her where her physical needs and also her social outlets could be handled so well. This lady was an example of the qualities needed to finish life with the luxury of being surrounded by loving family and caregivers.

Credit cannot be fully given to particular nursing homes. Another friend, Janet, joined me at a party given here to celebrate Mother's Day. She had visited here previously and was familiar with the happy atmosphere that surrounds us. Attending this Party made her realize how different the atmosphere was from the Retirement Home her mother is in. It is several states away and Mother moved there to be near more of her children and their families. She is living there in a beautiful facility near the children and their families. They are constantly trying to take care of her every need yet the Mother complains about their bad treatment of her and is constantly unhappy, which makes her family also unhappy. Too bad she didn't learn about finding her own happiness before now so she could appreciate the love and devotion everyone wants to give her. At this late date it is very difficult to make older people see how important they are to their families and how much they really are loved. It is another example of everyone's need to prepare their thinking so they can make their living space happier for now and for the others in their life.

Another friend, Alice, remembers her elderly aunt, who entered a nursing home years ago, and was very happy to be there. She appreciated the variety of the different personalities she could encounter now, especially having more men (male energy) there. Back in her own home she saw mostly women and many of them had similar personalities. Male friends and various types of women associations helped give her more reasons for being happy in a new location. We all are glad to hear stories of happiness, and to know it is possible to find it.

CHAPTER 12

Visions of Unconditional Love

When I first moved here, the prospect of living so closely with people whose minds were in decline (or sometimes just childish) really bothered me. Old fears raised their ugly heads and, because it seemed different from regular living, I looked around asking myself, "Will this place ever be satisfactory for me?"

At times like that, when stuck in destructive thinking and wanting to change, it is helpful to find a Role Model, someone who has the quality I desire. I found one and mentally started "walking in her shoes" and imitating her happy attitude. After successfully achieving that desirable quality, I was strong enough to go back to walking in my own shoes. There are several Role Models to imitate here and I watched them quickly bring order back when a resident had become disruptive and angry. It was from their patient-yet-firm attitudes that solved problems. Seeing loving-kindness in action was a wonderful example of Unconditional Love.

This reminded me of another very important experience of Unconditional Love that I had just a few weeks before moving here. It came in a vision, and now living in this atmosphere I have a chance to practice it in this lifetime. It was more than a single vision or a dream; it was action-packed and I was wide awake when it happened. Now, being here and seeing my change of attitude, I understood that it was another learning experience destined for me.

The love I began to feel for those elderly ones carried me back to the memory of that spiritual event (vision). It happened when I was still living in my apartment and sitting in the living room alone, wide awake but very tired. "Floaters" began to drift across my field of vision for a few minutes (this had happened to my eyes before so it was not a shock). Then the floaters took on different shapes in beautiful color combinations like orange with purple, pink with green, red with yellow. It gave me deep joy and appreciation as I sat back and watched the aesthetic beauty of the shapes and colors as they passed by. Suddenly, they increased in number and all the walls and even the ceiling were covered with more of those same brilliantly colored shapes. Then, each one became a perfectly arranged flower bouquet, each twisted around a garden limb. I'd never experienced anything so beautiful and it was hard to believe what I was seeing. This special show felt like a personal gift and I asked myself if my tiredness brought it about. Whatever it was, all of it made me feel tremendously blessed.

Finally, I reluctantly dragged my weary body back to my bedroom. After getting into bed and closing my eyes, curiosity made me open them again. What I saw was even more of the beautiful flowers on all those walls. Also, they were on the ceiling, which had risen eight feet in height and was covered with flowers just like the ones in the living room. The ceiling fan had changed to a huge chandelier, and was also flower covered.

Slowly, action began, just like in a movie. The bedroom became a picturesque town square. People appeared… none that I then recognized… they were all ages from babies playing on the grass to adults strolling by and talking to each other. No one even looked at me. Watching them I was overwhelmed with joy and felt great love for each one of that group of unknown individuals.

I had studied in *A Course in Miracles* about the great power of Unconditional Love. It explained that one's personal love can grow from being reserved for only a special few people to finally including *everyone*, and that state is called Unconditional Love. At the time I was greatly inspired by that idea and had tried to practice its all-inclusive feeling, but it seemed impossible for me then. Now, as I became aware of the strong love I felt for each of those individuals in the scene and everyone else I could recall, I knew this state of love was what I had been striving for and that awareness was so powerful that I literally sat up in bed and spoke these words **out loud**: "Thank you, God! This is it... what I feel right now... it must be the way You always feel about *us*! It is a state I have been wanting to reach, yet couldn't quite feel it in my conscious or unconscious mind, and now Unconditional Love is here in my heart!"

A little later I felt the weight of someone's arms pressed around me and saw that it was my Mother, and we silently embraced... then my Dad walked by... next came my Daughter also just walking by (all three had died years before). I was surprised that they didn't stop and talk to me instead of quickly disappearing. Even with that disappointment, I was too emotional to stop and question the "why" of it.

Now, writing about it, I can question why their visit was so silent and short. Perhaps their silence was symbolic of my "unconditionalness" for loving everyone exactly the same (like I had experienced in the Vision). Another explanation could be that I was viewing a scene from another dimension. Maybe God, Holy Spirit, or Whoever designed this family scene, was demonstrating a larger, stronger, overall Love than the more emotional way I would have greeted "special ones" on the level I live in now. This was quite an evolution in thinking, and it made me wonder if this intensity of Love would stay with me or fade away. I do know that now I have been able to change some critical judgments about people here at the Home, and that was possible because of experiencing Unconditional Love in the Vision.

It was a "Higher Power" that allowed me a peek into the Other Side and it has brought a newness and excitement that stays in my thoughts. Now, months have passed and I have discovered more of the deeper meaning of some of the details from the Visions that I didn't understand when first shown. Experiencing the Love was the most important, but there were more scenes that I described in my journal that night, and only now can look deeply into them. One vision was a scene created just off my bedroom. It looked like a very small room, only about 10' x 10', with eight foot high walls and no ceiling. This little room was totally packed full of rough bare branches covered with sharp looking briars. I had to walk through those briars and expected to be scratched to death. But I did it without hesitation, and was not scratched at all. I now understand that the briar-filled room represented the nursing home I would soon move into - *Briar*wood Nursing Home. The briars represented fears I had at first. In real life I did pass through symbolic briars to get to this nursing home experience, yet without any of the "scratches" and only the same fearless satisfaction I felt in the Vision.

After the briar-filled room came another scene back in the bedroom. To my left, the wall had changed to look like it was structured of old bricks. While observing it from my bed, the whole wall began to move toward me. This time I felt no fear, just watched it and when it got very close, I extended my hand toward it and it stopped. That made me laugh. The message may mean that the next time I am "up against a brick wall" I can stop it, without fear of being totally crushed.

Immediately after the brick wall vision, I thought I must remember all of this so decided to move back to the Dining Room Table where I could more comfortably make notes about it all. After I sat down at the table and began writing, I felt a presence.... I looked up and saw someone sitting beside me at the table, writing just as I was doing... and I knew it was another <u>Me</u>... exactly <u>Me</u>... only dressed slightly different. I was vaguely familiar with stories of "duplicate universes" and felt certain this was it, and for real! Unfortunately, I was so stunned at the possibility of viewing myself in another dimension that I jumped up and quickly turned off the light, left the Dining Room, and rushed back to the bedroom. My only thought was that this was something I had never, ever expected to experience, and it was just too New Age for me to understand. Now I regret that I couldn't stay and continue more of this fantastic experience. Overwhelmed, I fell into bed and was soon in deep sleep. The next morning when I woke and was reviewing the experience, I felt that there was much more to learn about this unseen world and I wanted to see more of it.

Two years have passed, and every bit of that vision is still clear in my memory. I am always aware of the feeling of Unconditional Love... even when I forget and almost lapse back into old feelings of separation and judgment of other people. Then, I forgive my humanness and everyone else's, and the Love stays with me.

A few days later as we gathered here in the Briarwood Dining Room, I looked at all the faces and felt genuine love for each person... not pity, but the comfort of sharing this latter part of life with everyone here. There is a sweetness to all being together at this particular time of life, but the *changes* caused by aging are drastic, even traumatic. Some oldsters may feel hurt by the changes but everyone here has the opportunity to overcome that. They may imagine a sense of separation from younger people because of age difference. Know that it is not yet a common practice for people to recognize and glorify this late period of life, but the time will soon come when all people, young and old, will give honor to those who have lived a life. All will celebrate their individual stories that show so much about Life.

CHAPTER 13

Mother Knows Best

There I was, a very young teenager sitting on the front porch shelling peas with Mother. The subject of a popular song (one of Mom's favorites, *AH Sweet Mystery of Life*) came up and I said, "I am tired of all those old songs and so many of the movies. They seem to be about one thing, Love...Love...Love." To my surprise, Mom stopped me and said, "Don't ever repeat words like that again. You must always remember that *Love is what makes the world go around! It is the greatest and most important power in the world*. I was shocked by the intensity of her remarks, and in my youthful ignorance I didn't immediately agree with her, but I never forgot her words. They remained with me through years of adversities and a deep curiosity about the unseen world.

Going through life we may get various concepts of God. We study the Bible, attend lectures, read books on world history and religions, and some people get so confused that all pictures (concepts) of God are wiped from their minds. But some humans (like me) really need some concept, or belief in a Higher Power as we travel thru the uncertainties of life, especially now with so many world changes happening.

My concept of God is in the simple phrase: *God is Love.* It gets me back to sanity as I remember what the "greatest power in the world" is...it *is* Love...and that is very obvious as I observe it in people every day. Most people are unaware of such a common trait that is so prevalent that it often is not *recognized* as Love. Lately, I have to walk with the help of a walker and never have to open a door or push through a crowd because when people see a person on a walker they just instinctively reach out to help them. Furthermore, it is not uncommon to hear about a person risking their own life to save a stranger from danger. And what about the many organizations of both volunteer and paid workers whose purpose in life is helping others! I received that firsthand during the fire at my apartment, and was shocked at the loving and efficient kindness that just surrounded me. It was the same instinctive Love that made three different drivers stop and offer to help me the day my car stalled... I would have gladly accepted their help if I hadn't just a moment before called Triple A. These offers for help occurred just a few minutes apart. I wonder if anyone realized it was their Love that made them act so quickly.

When responses of love are violated, it seems so rare that it is reported in the news, and the popular public reaction is like... "That proves that the whole world is getting worse. It is just too dangerous to even be alive... etc. etc." Such observations are caused by *blindness to all the love that is inherent in everyone and everything*. It is always there even when you don't see it.

Another element of love you will see is in Forgiveness. It happens so often and in so many small occurrences, that sometimes people see it as a *fault*. I saw a friend forget she was holding a grudge toward someone and when she saw him unexpectedly, greeted this opponent with a hug. Later she was serious when she said, "You just saw an example of my worst *fault* - not being able to hold a grudge for very long." If holding onto the grudge was a way to punish her offender, then her instinctive love had stopped her. It made me laugh at her "fault" and now I watch for more involuntary love,

And at this time in my life, it is great to be aware of all the facets of love. Just like Mother said, *Love is what makes the world go around! It is the greatest and most important power in the world.*

Thanks Mom!

CHAPTER 14

Humor

When life seems too grim to endure any longer, reach for a good dose of humor. They say "laughter is the best medicine" and when applied we can quit taking ourselves, and the world, so seriously… because laughter may make our good sense begin to come back. Here at the Home, daily life can become too routine and *laughter* can break that up and serve as a *lifeline,* so we grab hold of it and try to pass it on. Then we feel good knowing we have helped reduce suffering on the planet…like a comedian might feel when getting a laugh from the audience.

As you communicate with elders keep humor in mind, along with love. Some seniors are filled with so much pain that humor is impossible for them to give *or* receive. But please don't take your failure personally. Your love and devotion may be the only light in their lives at this time…as a caregiver you would never know it from their remarks to and about you. It can be a heavy time for you unless your Love is smart enough to know when to fall back on <u>silent</u> humor.

The Love/Humor theory can also work miracles for you in relationships between any age adults when Love is hidden by anger or blame. However, you must be careful then that your humor is not taken as disrespect, because that would worsen the situation. At such times it may be better to keep the funny part (that only you can see) to yourself. Nevertheless, your silent humor can generate healing qualities that lighten your own heart by showing you the Light in it all.

I had to resort to humor here at the Home one night. The doctor's orders then said I could take Tylenol "on request". Previously the orders were for Regular Doses "four times a day", but that seemed too much so I requested a change to "only on request". Then there was no problem as I received medicine when needed... except at night when I had pain and really needed the pills. That was because the night nurse was as grim as the night was dark, and she took her job seriously by questioning the intelligence of any resident (like me) knowing **what** they need and **when**.

When I asked her for Tylenol, she asked (suspiciously) where the pain was, I explained that it was in my legs which were cramping so severely I couldn't sleep. More questions... then she finally left the room for what seemed to me like an unnecessarily long wait and returned reluctantly with Tylenol. The same scenario was repeated two more nights... by then my pain became almost preferable to her Third Degree. So on the fourth night, when the same pain came on and made me call, she started the same quiz. Then, I just had to apply ridiculous humor. When she asked where my pain was I answered, "I don't have any pain! All I want is a Tylenol FIX... and hurry, because I need it so bad... and I looove that Tylenol fix... please, please hurry because without it I may have a seizure!" Bored with my antics, she turned and quickly returned with the (harmless) dosage. From then on, she silently granted my request without questions. It may have looked like *humor in extreme*, but since then, without my old resentment and anger, I can sleep away my leg pain. She no longer questions my requests, and now we have almost become friends.

Love is the answer to everything one considers too difficult... so I had to remember to keep Love in my thoughts, and if it seems to fail then I have to resort to another kind of Love... humor.

Another time I used humor to make myself relax so that I could fall asleep. While battling insomnia, I became aware of the tension-frown on my face and I couldn't make it go away. It reminded me of times I see frowning faces here at the Home and silently say to them, "Life is not easy, honey, but it would help if you would at least <u>try</u> to smile". Now I am forced to take back those thoughts because I was *trying* to smile and couldn't. Trying just wasn't enough to make me break into a smile that night. Then I searched for some humor! And what popped into my mind was the funny story my friend Mary Ellen told me that very day. Thinking about it broke up my tight facial frown as I laughed out loud. Here it is:

It happened in the grocery store parking lot. She had just arrived and was walking toward the store when she heard a demanding voice very close to her say, "Hold this!" It was a bottle thrust toward her by someone busily arranging groceries in the back of his car... head down... not looking up. Mary Ellen's reflex was just to follow orders, so she stood there and held the bottle. In a few minutes a woman appeared, apologized, and took the bottle from her. Then the "voice" spoke again, "Where were you? I thought this woman was you, and I told her to hold that bottle." The woman (wife) apologized again and before Mary Ellen could walk away... right then... the husband, quite obviously, *passed gas*. Mary Ellen flinched, and then turned and quickly left the scene... she'd had enough of their problems!

That scene really broke me up every time I thought of it. Laughter started and it was the medicine I needed right then to relax my body and giggle away the tension that had kept me awake for so long. Even if you are in pain, you may be able to make it lighter by remembering some silly phrase just for the sake of relaxation. It is such fun to be saved by humor... it works like turning on an electric light. It reminds me of a phrase I heard recently that made me smile all day. It was from a nurse here referring to her husband; she called him "my future ex-husband."

As you get "older" or at any age, friends who can make you laugh are the most valuable treasures you can have. When you were younger and busy with family and work maybe you couldn't spend enough time with them. But life changes, some die and some move away, leaving you now with plenty of free time and the need to find new friends to replace ones you lost. Now is the time to reach out with all the faith you can muster to find new people and start interviewing for who might qualify as your new friend. Think about what the requirements for such a person are...probably with as many similarities to yourself as possible, mainly in the category of a *sense of humor.* We are all individuals and appreciate our differences because they make life interesting. If that should show up and cause problems, just remember to laugh about them. Laugh at difficulties and always keep smiling.

Another tip: when first retiring, don't rush into moving to a new location too quickly. A few years ago I moved to start a new life far away. While there I made some valuable friends, but without the old ones from the old environment I felt I had "lost my identity". That is a hard lesson for a fragile ego—and you might know what I mean—so remember that during a move it is essential to keep a keen sense of humor. Then, overcoming any new challenge will be a great help for the ego. Add some silent or shared humor and you can get through life—laughing!

CHAPTER 15

Obsession with "Young"

There is a time, usually around Middle Age, when the fear of reaching old-age gets stronger. At the same time, the work of *looking young* intensifies and too often looking young becomes some middle-aged people's life ambition.

A friend told me that her husband had been angry all day after attending the funeral of his favorite high school teacher: "What happened there this morning that made you so angry?" she asked him. "Well, Miss Andrews was so well liked and there were a lot of old students my age there, and they looked so...broken down and old that it made me mad." That was what made her 70 year old husband unhappy for the rest of the day, and the whole household suffered from his depression. Ah...the worship of looking young...and the fear of losing it!

Well I, too, had taken looking old seriously and even felt a bit of fear at the prospects. It (fear) would intensify after receiving compliments for looking youthful! The praise felt so good it made me work harder and harder to keep it coming on by looking younger. Finally the effort got too demanding...trying to keep up with all the beauty aids while knowing I would soon become a loser in the challenge, so I lost interest and wanted out of the game. By then I had become frustrated because of all this country's obsession insisted that "beauty" had to be connected with "looking young". So, I have (sorta) gone to other interests, which seem more realistic. (But I must admit, I still try to look my best since the ego is still hovering around me.) Anyhow, my new interest is in information about Death and the events revealed about the "unseen world" which seems more interesting to me right now.

Like many of us, my first curiosity about the After Life came from discussions with people who had seen visions and had conversations with souls who had passed on. Back then those stories were fun and scary, but not taken seriously in religious circles or scientific investigation. Since then, there has been more research on the subject in medical settings and in the many books showing up on Best Seller Lists. Many of them are written by medical professionals and carry such titles as 'Life After Life', 'Near Death Experiences', 'Out of Body Travel' etc. I am very interested and have read many of them. Most important for me in all this is the positive proof it shows about real Life…that it really is *eternal,* even though it is *unseen* from here at this time. All we have are the many reports from people who have "been there" and returned to tell about it. I am so grateful to have this knowledge while still on This Side, and seeing the proof that Life is *eternal,* and is just one continuous *path of learning.* The lessons we encounter here teach us how to find more understanding, love and happiness. As the study continues, I look forward to learning more exciting truths about the After Life.

Many of the elderly don't seem very curious about these kinds of reports about the Other Side, or care about hearing any positive news of such discoveries. This lack of interest may indicate hidden fears of Death and their personal future in the next world (the unseen). Some fears are very difficult to overcome and when certain discussions cause older folks pain, then let it go and let them see your loving and optimistic viewpoint about your own latter life.

Don't be distracted away from such exciting information by worries about yourself "looking old" or "being old". We can't fully enjoy all the days of Life if we are half-ashamed of having lived a certain number of years. Do we have to apologize for having had a number of birthdays and try to make a joke of having the physical body that proves it? Why does that apology feel necessary? Stop now and take the time to review your life history. Admit your so-called mistakes and failures, then let your AGE prove to you that you have succeeded by living beyond those events and celebrate rather than apologize!

Practice really looking at everyone who has lived all the way up to Old Age. See their outer covering as the true evidence of success. Look at the very old wrinkled bodies and change your response from pity to respect. See real living that had to be experienced in order to create wrinkles. Admit that Life is not easy all the time for anyone. Would a military man or woman apologize for his/her medals of courage? Aging signs are also medals.

Celebrate the years, don't judge them. When you hear yourself saying, "I could have done better, or more with my life if…", know that that is your present day opinion and has nothing to do with your past. Back then you did do the best that those times and circumstances permitted considering your thinking and societies' opinions of the time. If you could have done more and better, you would have. So keep it up, make the age you are in the grand finale of having really LIVED A LIFE.

CHAPTER 16

Movin' On Up

When I was about to complete my first year of living here in a private room on the first floor, I knew I couldn't afford a private room much longer, and it would mean moving up to the second floor to live in a double room with a roommate. In other words, I would soon be moving <u>up</u>, but to my ego it felt more like moving <u>down</u>. It (ego) said that this move would let the world know I had run out of money and my future would be living from the goodness of Medicaid, Medicare, and friends (who still cared). I envisioned that when visitors walked thru the Second Floor Day Room crowded with residents in various states of health, to get to my new room, they would think I must be *depressed*, instead of in my usual happy state. Of course, all these were the typical imaginary scenes that ego (pride) creates. But really, who cares! My old fearful self just has to erupt at times. On moving day, while riding upstairs with Mary, one of the executives who wanted to comfort me, said, "There have been others who have moved up here from the first floor, then later said they really preferred living up here *more* than downstairs. My reply was unenthusiastic, but my thought was... THAT'S NOT ME... NEVER!

For the first few days I didn't have a roommate in the new room so the move was accomplished easily after making things fit into a slightly smaller space. I dreaded going to the Second Floor Dining Room but I remembered having had similar (mistaken) dreads about group-eating a year ago, and it made this time much easier. Luckily I was given a permanent seat at a table with three other ladies, much like myself, and they were very comfortable to be with. They helped me to get over the sadness of leaving my downstairs tablemates and other friends and employees from down there. That ego-pride thing was exaggerated; the new people and the surroundings were just as attractive up here.

Pretty soon the change was so successful that I questioned my loyalty about leaving my old first-floor friends because I was soon satisfied. However, adjusting to life with various roommates was another story. It was a learning opportunity that was valuable because... I guess, because it *was* so difficult.

I have always valued my private time and didn't know how I'd adjust to sharing a space with someone. Thru the years I had learned the importance of Love... I knew that it could overcome any difficulty... so now I would have an opportunity to practice Love with whoever shared that space, and my peace and happiness would naturally follow. (This thought later reminded me of the extreme value of practicing conscious thinking before meeting difficult circumstances.)

The Higher Power must have thought I needed more of that practice because in less than a year <u>six</u> different roommates have moved through this room. The first person was recovering after surgery and here only to take physical therapy so her stay was temporary. We were each considerate of the other's privacy but took time for some serious discussions which we both enjoyed. She left appreciating it here so much that she came back several times to visit us. I was confident then that, with the right attitude, living with a roommate was easy.

Not so with the next four! They each were put here against their will and fought to get out. Their only weapon was refusing to cooperate with everyone who tried to help them. I had a chance to watch how the staff returned anger and abusive outbursts with positive patience and, in those circumstances, my job was to observe and follow suit. I still wonder what the lives of those elderly women had been before coming here, and why it was so impossible for them to cope with this life change. It can be a difficult change for some but being *at war* with the world is futile, it's like a disease that takes away their good sense and leaves them in an infantile state with refusal to accept help. It was better when family came to visit; they usually just quietly complained then and saved heavy emotions for caregivers and roommates. One of these souls met Death while in this room, another stayed less than a day, and then a family member moved her to another room without giving me time to feel guilty for any lack of hospitality. The next fought her way to a vacancy down the hall. Now fortunately, the most recent one has been here for several weeks and we both appreciate the arrangement, and don't want it to change.

I can honestly say that peace now reigns for me in this room and also in the Dining Hall. When outsiders and even close friends say they don't believe me, and think my happiness is just a brave front… well, I understand because I didn't believe Mary either that day she told me some people liked it better living here on the Second Floor than on the First Floor. Now reluctantly, I agree with her about the move I had to make. I am more aware now when I get a negative feeling and quickly find the blessing in it and usually a positive change happens. So, I can still claim a feeling of happiness wherever I am. The dreaded move was a blessing after all, and actually I am "Movin' On Up" in many ways.

P.S. There may be more to learn! Now there's a rumor that there will soon be a vacancy back on the First Floor, and I am scheduled to get it. My reaction was a shock! Do I really want to give up my Second Floor home? Loving so many people makes me never want to leave anyone, ever! How can I ever make the real EXIT?

CHAPTER 17

Exit

Listen to the final crash of thunder as the storm disappears into the distance. That sound is the great final "Amen" after a mighty chorus of wind and rain has moved on. Now we feel safe under the calm sky with only an echo of its passing might rumbling farther down the road. We feel safe under the fresh clear sky and question why those distant rumblings don't make us fearful of the storm's return. Could it be that we finally learned from past experiences that blessings always follow fearful situations?

The Storm is a hologram of Life and Death, ending with those diminishing sounds of a great clearing. The storm was an example of Life passing on from one situation to another, not an ending but a passage. The thunder relates to the trauma that the surviving ones feel at the death of a loved one. Now visualize the clearing sky as the gentle wind exits the dying one from his/her old location and enters them onto a more beautiful location into the loving arms of friends and family they haven't seen for years. He/she is treated with honor and great respect for having gotten thru this recent Life. He loves this place and wants to stay and never leave. His only regret is the grief experienced by people he has left back home. He knows that if they could see how happy his life is now, they would not feel such grief for his passing or sadness for themselves because they are lonely now.

Most older people and many others, can't permit themselves to learn any new information on death and dying, so they continue to stay confused about it. In their resentment and feelings of separation from younger generations, it makes the subject of death difficult for families to discuss. If and when they can, it helps for both age groups to discuss death in an optimistic way... showing respect for past beliefs, yet with a new appreciation of the proof of a better life in the future. For some reasons, this information was hidden from religious teaching for hundreds of years, but we are coming to a new age of global awareness. New books and films that give evidence of life after death are gradually being seen in Religious Circles, so in the foreseeable future much of the fear of death will slip away.

Just in the past few years there have been many reports of Afterlife experiences from people who were clinically dead then came back to tell about the experiences they had on the other side. This is not something new. The history of great spiritual leaders in the Bible and other religious texts tell of their exploration and observation of the spiritual dimensions of reality. When we separate from our earthly bodies we are following in their footsteps in a new environment of eternity. All these reports make me feel more certain that life is eternal and joyful. It seems to me that the religious and scientific perspectives about eternal life are finding more common ground. I find that tremendously exciting and am eager to see what new learning develops.

All of the positive lessons I learned before and since living in this Nursing Home have made me appreciate and enjoy these latter years. My younger years hold precious memories, but I don't yearn for a repeat of them. My present goal is helping to eliminate the fears that people of all ages carry… of reaching old age, perhaps living in a nursing home, and finally having to face the unknown experiences of death. Working through such fears may take some time, but it will be time well spent because we will get a bigger picture of our power and possibilities in Life now and in our future Life. An open mind will pave the way to new ways of seeing and thinking.

Bon voyage to all of us!

Appreciation

It is a joy to acknowledge those who contributed much time and talent to the completion of this book. For their tireless efforts to make the computer cooperate, I give loving thanks to Lynn Hopkins and Elliott Sorge; to Kathy Wagenknecht much appreciation for creating the Blog (http://waytonursinghome.blogspot.com); to Liz Lehmans for editing and putting the book pages together; to Don Meyers for designing the book cover; and also much love and appreciation to Alice Holeman, Rebecca Hochradel, and to all my other adopted daughters for helping to keep me alive.

Dear Reader,

I would love to hear your comments about the book. You can email me at:

dorisgates1808@comcast.net